FRENCH POEMS IN ENGLISH VERSE, 1850-1970

by

Dorothy Brown Aspinwall

The Scarecrow Press, Inc.
Metuchen, N.J.   1973

Library of Congress Cataloging in Publication Data

Aspinwall, Dorothy Brown, 1910-   comp.
  French poems in English verse, 1850-1970.

  English and French.
  1. French poetry--19th century. 2. French poetry--
20th century. 3. French poetry--Translations into
English. 4. English poetry--Translations from French.
I. Title.
PQ1183.A8   841'.008   73-1782
ISBN 0-8108-0599-5

Copyright 1973 by Dorothy Brown Aspinwall

To the memory of

Jacques and Marie Lusseyran

ACKNOWLEDGMENTS

The following permissions are gratefully acknowledged.

To reprint and translate:

LIBRAIRIE ERNEST FLAMMARION
"Cette fille, elle est morte" by Paul Fort from <u>Ballades Françaises,</u> Vol. I, 1896.
EDITIONS GALLIMARD
"Le Temps d'un éclair" by Paul Eluard from <u>La Vie immédiate,</u> 1932. "Psaume XLI" by Patrice de <u>La Tour du Pin</u> from <u>Les Psaumes,</u> 1938. "Dans la nuit" by Henri Michaux from <u>L'Espace</u> du dedans. 1944. "Plein ciel" by Jules Supervielle from <u>1939-1945.</u> "Le Dernier Poème" by Robert Desnos from <u>Domaine public,</u> 1945. "Pour toi mon amour" and "Rue de Seine" by Jacques Prévert from <u>Paroles,</u> 1946. "Le Loriot" by René Char from <u>Fureur et mystère,</u> 1948. "Lettre du vingt-six juin" by <u>Philippe</u> Jaccottet from <u>Poésie,</u> 1946-1967.
EDITIONS DE LA MAISON FRANÇAISE
"Le Lilas blanc," "Le Rossignol," and "Le Chant du coq" by Mathilde Monnier from <u>Dispersion,</u> 1942.
EDITIONS MERCURE DE FRANCE
"Odelette I," "Odelette IV," "Odelette XI," "Pour la Porte des exilés," and "Elégie double" by Henri de Régnier from <u>Les Jeux rustiques et divins,</u> 1897. "Voeu" by Henri de Régnier from <u>Les Médailles d'argile,</u> 1900. "Chanson" and "La Voix" by Henri de Régnier from <u>La Sandale ailée,</u> 1906. "Bascule" by Pierre Reverdy from <u>Sources du vent,</u> 1929.
EDITIONS SEGHERS
"S.O.S." and "Rose de Sang" by Yvan Goll from <u>L'Antirose,</u> 1965.
EDITIONS DU SEUIL
"Canto XXV" by Pierre Emmanuel from <u>XX Cantos,</u> 1942.
IMPRIMERIE L. VANMELLE
"Chanson" by Maurice Maeterlinck from <u>Douze Chansons,</u> 1896.

Acknowledgments v

    To reprint the French:

EDITIONS GALLIMARD
    "Le Pont Mirabeau" by Guillaume Apollinaire from <u>Alcools,</u> 1913.

    To translate into English:

NEW DIRECTIONS
    "Le Pont Mirabeau" by Guillaume Apollinaire.

    To reprint the following translations:

<u>Poet Lore</u>
    "For the Gate of Exiles," spring 1946; "A Girl Speaks" and "The Voice," spring 1947; "Tre Fila d'Oro," "Icibas," "The Bluebird," "Odelette I," "Odelette IV," "Odelette XI," and "Double Elegy," summer 1947; and "Wish," autumn 1948.

The following translations first appeared in:

<u>The Lantern</u>
    "Song" [de Régnier], May-June 1941; "Noël Sceptique," November-December 1941.
<u>The Husk</u>
    "Song" [Maeterlinck], October 1947.
<u>Mele</u>
    "Seesaw," January 1966; "The Nightingale," August 1966; "High in the Sky," May 1967; "Dawn," November 1967; "S.O.S.," January 1969; "Blood Rose," April 1970; "Canto XXV," February 1971; and "Letter of June 26," November 1971.

The translated extract of Péguy's <u>The portico of the mystery of the second virtue</u> is from the edition of the complete poem, published by The Scarecrow Press, Metuchen, N.J., copyright 1970 by Dorothy Brown Aspinwall.

TABLE OF CONTENTS

Acknowledgments	iv
Preface	xi
Notes on the Poets	xiii
Théophile Gautier	xiii
Noël	24
Noël	25
Charles Leconte de Lisle	xiii
Tre fila d'oro	26
Three Gold Strands	27
Charles Baudelaire	xiii
La Cloche fêlée	28
The Cracked Bell	29
Recueillement	30
Meditation	31
Alphonse Daudet	xiv
L'Oiseau bleu	32
The Bluebird	33
Sully Prudhomme	xiv
Ici-bas	34
Here Below	35
Paul Verlaine	xiv
Le Bruit des cabarets	36
The Noise of Cabarets	37
Arthur Rimbaud	xv
Aube	38
Dawn	39
Stéphane Mallarmé	xv
Brise marine	40
Sea Breeze	41

Jean Moréas	xv
Une Jeune fille parle	42
A Girl Speaks	43
Emile Verhaeren	xvi
Chaque heure où je songe	44
As I Muse Each Hour	45
Les Heures claires XXIX	46
Shining Hours	47
Maurice Maeterlinck	xvi
Chanson	48
Song	49
Paul Fort	xvi
Cette fille, elle est morte	50
Ballad of a Dead Girl	51
Henri de Régnier	xvi
Odelette I	52
Odelette I	53
Odelette IV	54
Odelette IV	55
Odelette XI	56
Odelette XI	57
Elégie double	58
Double Elegy	59
Pour la Porte des exilés	62
For the Gate of Exiles	63
Voeu	64
Wish	65
Chanson	66
Song	67
La Voix	68
The Voice	69
Jules Laforgue	xvii
Noël sceptique	70
Noël Sceptique	71
Charles Péguy	xvii
Le Porche du mystère de la deuxième vertu (extrait)	72
The Portico of the Mystery of the Second Virtue (extract)	73
Guillaume Apollinaire	xvii
Le Pont Mirabeau	76
Mirabeau Bridge	77

Pierre Reverdy	xviii
Bascule	78
Seesaw	79
Paul Eluard	xviii
Le Temps d'un éclair	80
In a Flash	81
Patrice de La Tour du Pin	xviii
Psaume XLI	82
Psalm XLI	83
Pierre Emmanuel	xix
Canto XXV	84
Canto XXV	85
Mathilde Monnier	xix
Le Lilas blanc	86
The White Lilac	87
Le Rossignol	88
The Nightingale	89
Le Chant du coq	90
Cockcrow	91
Henri Michaux	xix
Dans la nuit	92
In the Night	93
Robert Desnos	xx
Le Dernier poème	94
The Last Poem	95
Jules Supervielle	xx
Plein ciel	96
High in the Sky	97
Jacques Prévert	xx
Pour toi mon amour	98
For You My Love	99
Rue de Seine	100
Rue de Seine	101
René Char	xx
Le Loriot	104
The Oriole	105

Yvan Goll	xxi
S. O. S.	106
S. O. S.	107
Rose de sang	108
Blood Rose	109
Philippe Jaccottet	xxi
Lettre du vingt-six juin	110
Letter of June 26th	111
Note About the Translator	113

PREFACE

"If the package is disposable, it is not a poem." This is the way Mr. Stanley Burnshaw in The Poem Itself [New York: Holt, Rinehart and Winston, 1960] distinguishes between prose and poetry. In the twentieth century poetry need not, in fact usually does not, rhyme; in the twentieth century poetry need not, in fact usually does not, have a rhythm system; that is, a reader cannot foresee the length of the coming line or the position of the stresses. In other words, free verse is fashionable. Nor can the reader distinguish a poem from prose by considering the disposition of the words on the page: there are prose poems. The dividing line is hard to draw. Yet there is a difference, and Mr. Burnshaw's criterion is accurate and comprehensive.

If, then, a poem is a poem by reason of its form, all the literal, word-for-word translations of French poems are travesties.

In the present volume of translations of both traditional and modern French poems, the translator has tried to preserve the form as well as the thought and the emotion of the originals. A classic alexandrine--un tétramètre--becomes anapestic hexameter; rimes platés, end rhymed couplets; sounds repeated for their musical effect are imitated by consonantal or vocalic alliteration.

Whenever an impasse was reached, the translator applied the priorities advocated by Alexander Fraser Tytler in his Essay on the Principles of Translation [London, ca. 1790, p. 9]:

1. ... the translator should give a complete transcript of the ideas of the original work.
2. ... the style and manner of writing should be of the same character with that of the original.
3. ... the translation should have all the ease of original composition.

No claim is made that the poets represented here are the greatest of their age, for there are notable omissions and several unusual inclusions. Nor are the poems chosen necessarily the best-known of each author. No two anthologists would ever select identical contents. In the case of an anthologist who is also translating, a further factor is added to the element of personal choice: the translatableness (cf. Webster!) of a poem. For example, it seems impossible to come anywhere near doing justice to "Bateau ivre" or "Le Cimetière marin," yet these are undeniably more important than Henri de Régnier's graceful "Odelettes" that slip so easily into English clothing.

It is the translator's modest hope that this volume will give the non-French reader close contact with some of France's great poets.

> Dorothy Brown Aspinwall
> University of Hawaii
> Honolulu, Hawaii
> February 1972

NOTES ON THE POETS

THEOPHILE GAUTIER (1811-1872)

Gautier described himself thus: "I am a man for whom the outside world exists." He was an artist who painted with words and who valued perfection of form above all else. Especially in the later poems of Emaux et Camées which were to establish him as the precursor of the Art for Art's Sake school of poets, called Parnassians, we find almost no lyricism, imagination, or philosophy, none of the qualities that had distinguished the Romantics. In "Noël" one has the impression that Gautier is with great accuracy transposing into words some ancient picture of the Nativity.

CHARLES LECONTE DE LISLE (1818-1894)

Leconte de Lisle, born on an island in the Indian Ocean now named Réunion, settled permanently in France in 1845. At the time of his death, although still almost unknown to the public, he was considered by other poets and by critics as the leader of the Art for Art's Sake school and the greatest French poet of his day.

Haunted by the problem of man's mortality, Leconte de Lisle studied many of the world's religions only to conclude that existence itself is an evil. Because he believed that the emotions of an individual are of little importance in the vast human scheme, he did not express his despair directly, and his poems often seem marble cold. The lyric given here is obviously not typical of his work.

CHARLES BAUDELAIRE (1821-1867)

Les Fleurs du mal (Flowers of Evil), the collection from which these sonnets are taken, has had a dominating influence on all French poetry written since its publication. It was Baudelaire who, after reading Poe, began using words for their musical and emotional value rather than for the ideas that they represent. It was Baudelaire's famous sonnet, "Correspondances," that expressed the theory that the sensations of sight, sound, touch, and smell can evoke each other because they are different interpretations of the same phenomena.

The poet was an extremely unhappy man: he longed for "order and beauty" and felt that man's life ought to be directed by his will. His own will power was not sufficiently strong to keep him from excesses of every sort. His dissipated life, particularly the use of drugs, prevented him from realizing his ideal in his writing. In "La Cloche fêlée" he tells us how painful is this feeling of impotence and sterility. In "Recueillement" he enjoys a mood of nostalgic regret in company with his suffering, which he personifies as a woman or a girl-child.

ALPHONSE DAUDET (1840-1897)

Daudet began his literary career at the age of eighteen with a volume of verse, Les Amoureuses. It was soon overshadowed by his famous short stories, novels, and plays. His artistic excellence, his gay wit, and his ready compassion made this writer from the south of France popular with both the general public and the intellectual elite.

SULLY PRUDHOMME (1839-1907)

In the last century Sully Prudhomme was highly esteemed for his long philosophical poems. Today he is little read; if his work is represented in an anthology, the poem selected is almost always "Le Vase." "Ici-bas," given here, is a delicate, restrained lyric. One feels a simple, sincere wistfulness in the polished lines.

PAUL VERLAINE (1844-1896)

"Le Bruit des Cabarets," written for Verlaine's fiancée, is one of the few happy poems of this weak and melancholy man.

Although Verlaine began to write under the influence of the Parnassians, his work is far removed from their ideal of perfect objectivity. His poems are always simple, sincere, and subjective. He excels in evoking an elusive sensation or a fleeting emotion in an original melodious form.

Notes on the Poets

ARTHUR RIMBAUD (1854-1891)

As a brilliant rebellious boy in Charleville, Rimbaud ran away to Paris five times. On the fifth attempt he was befriended by Verlaine who had been greatly impressed by the young boy's poem "Bateau ivre." Between the age of fifteen and nineteen Rimbaud was a poetic genius; then he renounced poetry completely for a life of commercial adventure in Abyssinia. It was Verlaine who published Illuminations from manuscripts saved by friends. This volume of prose poems was to influence all future French poets.

STEPHANE MALLARME (1842-1898)

Mallarmé began to write as a member of the Parnassian group and always retained its ideal of craftsmanship. After 1884, however, he became the recognized leader of the Symbolists. As such, he gently expounded the new doctrine of aesthetics every Tuesday evening to the principal poets of the new generation. He advocated and wrote an intellectual type of poetry without the elements of sensation and emotion. In his poems he never explains the symbols he uses, nor develops any idea at length; he relies on the music of his words to evoke the reader's dreams. His poetry is pure language built on nothing.

Although most of Mallarmé's work is obscure, and voluntarily so, "Brise marine" tells us clearly of the poet's longing to exchange humdrum happiness for some mysterious adventure.

JEAN MOREAS (1856-1910)

Moréas is the nom de plume of a Greek poet who, after joining the French Symbolists, became the founder of a neo-classical school.

"Une Jeune fille parle" resembles the "Chansons de Toile" of the Middle Ages, songs that women used to sing as they sat in a group weaving or embroidering. The subject--man's inconstancy--is typical, as are the use of dialogue, the great simplicity, the religious reference in the refrain, the note of sadness. Several archaic words and the old-fashioned flowers enhance the medieval atmosphere.

EMILE VERHAEREN (1855-1916)

This powerful and original Belgian poet speaks more directly to the reader than do the Symbolist poets. Most of his work shows his deep concern for humble people faced by want and war. The lyrics that follow are of a different sort: they celebrate his unusually happy marriage.

MAURICE MAETERLINCK (1862-1949)

Maeterlinck was a Belgian poet who wrote of the mystery that pervades our daily existence in plays, of which the best known are The Bluebird and Pelléas and Mélisande, and in two slim volumes of poems.

Convinced that man is incapable of acting on the obscure forces that govern his destiny, Maeterlinck counsels an attitude of proud resignation and love for one's fellow sufferers.

He received the Nobel prize for literature in 1911.

PAUL FORT (1872-1960)

All his adult life Fort sang the legends, folkways, and charm of the French provinces. Most of the poems in the many volumes of his French Ballads are printed like prose although they employ rhythm and often rhyme. Their true originality lies in the informality of the language. Later poets such as Apollinaire and Desnos thought of Paul Fort as one of the early exponents of popular poetry.

HENRI DE REGNIER (1864-1936)

Although Régnier's poetic style is extremely varied, evolving from romantic tendencies through symbolism to neo-classicism, he is considered a Symbolist. In fact, his election to the Académie Française in 1911 marked the official recognition of Symbolism. The public was able to accept his new rhythms, his free verse, and his extensive use of symbols, because of the strongly traditional elements in his work: his conservative language and syntax, his clarity, his constant references to Greek antiquity, his grave aristocratic tone.

Notes on the Poets

JULES LAFORGUE (1860-1887)

Born of French parents in Montevideo, Laforgue at the age of six was sent to school in France. (The ship in which he sailed took seventy-five days to reach Bordeaux!) After completing his studies he lived precariously until 1881, dividing his time between his writing and a small post as secretary. Then, for five years, he was reader to the Empress Augusta of Germany. Next followed his romantic marriage to a penniless English girl and his death from tuberculosis a year later.

Laforgue's melancholy irony is often charming. Although his work does not rank with that of Baudelaire, Mallarmé, or Verlaine, it is nevertheless important: he is credited (along with Gustave Kahn) with inventing free verse, and he was among the first poets to introduce a conversational tone and syncopated rhythms. Ezra Pound and T. S. Eliot were impressed and influenced by him.

The poem given in this collection is among Laforgue's most traditional verse.

CHARLES PEGUY (1873-1914)

Péguy was proud of the fact that he came of peasant stock. After studying on scholarships at the Lycée of Orleans, the city of his birth, and at two lycées in Paris and the Ecole Normale Supérieure, he abandoned plans for an academic career to open a socialist bookstore near the Sorbonne.

In 1900 he founded a sort of magazine called <u>Les Cahiers de la Quinzaine</u> of which each issue was a complete book. In these issues he or one of his illustrious contributors usually discussed philosophical or social problems, but occasionally Péguy devoted a <u>Cahier</u> to one of his long poems.

The extract given here comes from Series XIII, no. 4, a long monologue in which God speaks through the voice of a young nun.

GUILLAUME APOLLINAIRE (1880-1918)

A friend of many Cubist painters, including Picasso and Modigliani, Apollinaire wanted to renew poetic expression by substituting for the vagueness of the Symbolists the geometrical reconstruction of reality employed by the Cubists. He coined the term Surrealism. In <u>Alcools,</u> his first volume of poems, he dispensed with punctuation which he considered useless, esteeming that the rhythm and the pause in a line of verse are the true punctuation. In his second volume, called <u>Calligrammes,</u> the poems are arranged so that the lines form a design. Despite his daring innovations in form, his work is often in the romantic tradition: he reveals his personal suffering.

"Le Pont Mirabeau" was addressed to the painter, Marie Laurencin, who was at the center of Apollinaire's sentimental life for five years. The refrain increases our impression of long weary waiting and of disillusionment.

PIERRE REVERDY (1889-1960)

In 1924 the Surrealists termed Pierre Reverdy "the greatest living poet." Six years later he withdrew from the artistic revolution in Paris to devote the remainder of his days to meditation on life and art in a humble house near the Benedictine monastery at Solesmes.

The poem "Bascule," like many of Reverdy's poems, records a drama, a moment of mental struggle in which the boundaries of exterior reality seem to dissolve. Notice how the spacing of lines on the page suggests the motion of a seesaw.

PAUL ELUARD (1895-1952)

In 1942 Eluard became internationally known through the publication in many different languages of his poem called "Liberté" or "Seule Pensée." As does the poem given in the present work, it spoke directly to people, for Eluard believed that poetry ought to be written for humanity. As a young man he had collaborated with Dadaists and Surrealists, but after 1934 he found his own style--a marvelous combination of simplicity and mystery.

PATRICE DE LA TOUR DU PIN (1911-   )

It was Jules Supervielle who "discovered" the twenty-year-old La Tour du Pin and arranged for one of his poems to be published in <u>La Nouvelle Revue Française.</u>
Since his student days his whole life has been devoted to poetry and to the service of God. After four years spent as a prisoner of the Germans, he retired to his country estate where he lives happily with his wife and daughters in

virtual seclusion.
   Some critics, notably Pierre de Boisdeffre, rate the work of La Tour du Pin with the very best of this century. [see Une Anthologie vivante de la littérature d'aujourd'hui, Paris: Librairie Académique Perrin, 1966; p. 768].

PIERRE EMMANUEL (1916-   )

   Emmanuel is a serious philosophical poet who was instrumental in leading the new generation of writers away from Surrealism. Since the war all his work is inspired by Catholicism; he affirms the existence of God, the divine nature of man, and the poet's role as interpreter of the present and the eternal.
   Although there were twenty poems in the original edition of XX Cantos, there are over two hundred in the complete edition, which is entitled Chansons du dé à coudre (Songs of the Thimble).

MATHILDE-ANNA MONNIER (1887-1967)

   Monnier, who usually wrote under the name of Thyde Monnier, began at an early age to compose poems, short stories, and plays. It was not until she was fifty that her name became known to the general public through the publication of a novel.
   Born in Marseilles, she spent almost her entire life in the south of France.

HENRI MICHAUX (1899-   )

   Born in Belgium, Michaux became a French citizen in 1955. Much of his life has been spent wandering around the world seeking escape. His life, his writing, and his painting show a nature in perpetual revolt against the absurdity of life, against reality, against death, and the need to create a private world. He seems to feel threatened on all sides and to write in order to exorcise his obsessions. One of his means of defense is the disorganization of the universe by the imagination aided by mescaline.
   "Dans la nuit" is an invocation and an exorcism in which the repetition of certain sounds is more important than the exact sense of the words.

ROBERT DESNOS (1900-1945)

After practically idolizing André Breton, the French theoretician of the Surrealist movement, Desnos abruptly left the group in 1921 to return to a more traditional type of poetry.

Having joined the Résistance in 1940, he was arrested by the Gestapo in February 1944 and died of typhus in a concentration camp in April of the following year.

"Le Dernier poème," written just before his death, was entrusted to a Czech student to be delivered to Youki, the poet's wife.

JULES SUPERVIELLE (1884-1960)

The life of Supervielle was divided between Uruguay, where he was born of French parents, and Paris, where he studied as a young man and spent his last fourteen years. Perhaps his many ocean crossings helped to develop in him the cosmic sense that is apparent in much of his work.

Supervielle belongs to no school of poets. He distinguished himself from the Surrealists by an earnest, humble desire to communicate to others his sympathy for everything in the universe. He has been praised as the most imaginative of twentieth-century French poets.

JACQUES PREVERT (1900-)

Prévert was famous for his film scenarios, and his poems were recited in night-clubs long before his first volume of verse, Paroles, appeared in 1945. He is one of France's most popular poets. His revolt against all conventions and his original associations of ideas have particularly endeared him to the young. When exposing sham and injustice he can be biting and bitter.

RENE CHAR (1907-)

Char has twice emerged from his country solitude near Avignon: first, in order to collaborate with André Breton and Paul Eluard and other surrealist poets, and, second, during the Occupation to take an active role in the Résistance.

The three lines of "Le Loriot" tell us by means of startling images how he felt on the fateful day when France declared war on Germany.

Notes on the Poets

YVAN GOLL (1891-1950)

An Alsatian whose first poems were written in German, Goll, a pacifist, took refuge in Switzerland during the First World War and in the United States during the Second.

With his wife, Claire, he collaborated on several volumes of lyrics including one published after his death, <u>L'Antirose</u>, from which come the two poems in this collection.

PHILIPPE JACCOTTET (1925-)

Born in Switzerland, Jaccottet has spent his adult years in Paris and in Grignan (Drôme). In addition to his fame as a poet, he has earned an enviable reputation as a translator and literary critic.

Jaccottet speaks directly to the reader without exaggeration, without guile, of his quest for truth, his efforts to understand the relationship of the limited and the Limitless.

THE POEMS
AND THEIR TRANSLATIONS

NOEL
Théophile Gautier

Le ciel est noir, la terre est blanche;
--Cloches, carillonnez gaîment!--
Jésus est né;--la Vierge penche
Sur lui son visage charmant

Pas de courtines festonnées
Pour préserver l'enfant du froid;
Rien que les toiles d'araignées
Qui pendent des poutres du toit.

Il tremble sur la paille fraîche,
Ce cher petit enfant Jésus,
Et pour l'échauffer dans sa crèche
L'âne et le boeuf soufflent dessus.

La neige au chaume coud ses franges,
Mais sur le toit s'ouvre le ciel
Et, tout en blanc, le choeur des anges
Chante aux bergers: "Noël! Noël!"

<u>Emaux et Camées.</u> 1852

NOEL

The sky is dark, the earth is white;
O bells, ring out, peal loud with joy!
Jesus is born; the Virgin bends
Her lovely face above her boy.

No curtains draped around his bed
To guard the sleeping child from cold;
Nothing but spider webs hang there
From rafters blackened and old.

He shivers on the chilly straw,
This little holy babe, and here
To warm him in his manger crib
The ox and ass stand breathing near.

The snow sews fringes on the thatch,
Above the roof the skies reveal
A white-robed angel choir that sings
Carols of joy as shepherds kneel.

TRE FILA D'ORO
Leconte de Lisle

Là-bas, sur la mer, comme l'hirondelle,
Je voudrais m'enfuir, et plus loin encor!
Mais j'ai beau vouloir, puisque la cruelle
A lié mon coeur avec trois fils d'or.

L'un est son regard, l'autre son sourire,
Le troisième, enfin, est la lèvre en fleur;
Mais je l'aime trop, c'est un vrai martyre:
Avec trois fils d'or elle a pris mon coeur!

Oh! si je pouvais dénouer ma chaîne!
Adieu, pleurs, tourments; je prendrais l'essor.
Mais non, non! mieux vaut mourir à la peine
Que de vous briser, ô mes trois fils d'or.

<u>Pièces diverses.</u> 1855

THREE GOLD STRANDS

As swallows glide o'er white waves' curl,
I long to flee to distant lands;
My wish is vain: a cruel girl
Has bound my heart with three gold strands.

One is her glance, and one her smile,
The third her ruby lips apart;
I am a martyr to her wile:
With three gold strands she snared my heart.

Oh! if I could untie my chain!
Forget despair, my wings unfold!
No, no! much better die in pain
Than sever you, my strands of gold.

LA CLOCHE FELEE
Charles Baudelaire

Il est amer et doux, pendant les nuits d'hiver,
D'écouter, près du feu qui palpite et qui fume,
Les souvenirs lointains lentement s'élever
Au bruit des carillons qui chantent dans la brume.

Bienheureuse la cloche au gosier vigoreux
Qui, malgré sa vieillesse, alerte et bien portante,
Jette fidèlement son cri religieux,
Ainsi qu'un vieux soldat qui veille sous la tente!

Moi, mon âme est fêlée, et lorsqu'en ses ennuis
Elle veut de ses chants peupler l'air froid des nuits,
Il arrive souvent que sa voix affaiblie

Semble le râle épais d'un blessé qu'on oublie
Au bord d'un lac de sang, sous un grand tas de morts,
Et qui meurt, sans bouger, dans d'immenses efforts!

Les Fleurs du mal. 1857

THE CRACKED BELL

It is bitter and sweet on a cold wintry night,
By the side of a hearth with a smoldering log,
To listen to memories ascend in slow flight
To the tune of the chimes as they sing through the fog.

O how blest is the bell with a powerful throat
That in spite of its age, sound, alert, confident,
Still proclaims in religious devotion each note,
Like a sentinel keeping watch in a tent!

When my soul that is cracked and is burdened with care
Is impatient to fill with its songs the night air,
Its enfeebled old voice is most likely to sound

Like the croak of a wounded man left on the ground
Overlooked, underneath a red heap of the slain,
And who dies, still, inert, with great effort and strain.

RECUEILLEMENT
Charles Baudelaire

Sois sage, O ma Douleur, et tiens-toi plus tranquille.
Tu réclamais le Soir; il descend; le voici:
Une atmosphère obscure enveloppe la ville,
Aux uns portant la paix, aux autres le souci.

Pendant que des mortels la multitude vile,
Sous le fouet du Plaisir, ce bourreau sans merci,
Va cueillir des remords dans la fête servile,
Ma Douleur, donne-moi la main; viens par ici

Loin d'eux. Vois se pencher les défuntes Années,
Sur les balcons du ciel, en robes surannées;
Surgir du fond des eaux le Regret souriant;

Le Soleil moribond s'endormir sous une arche,
Et, comme un long linceul traînant à l'Orient,
Entends, ma chère, entends la douce Nuit qui marche.

Les Fleurs du mal. 1857

MEDITATION

Be good, dear Sorrow, and sit quietly.
You clamored for Dusk; it is everywhere:
The city is bathed in obscurity;
To some it brings peace, to others grave care.

While, driven by merciless Pleasure's goads,
The masses of base-souled humanity
Haste to harvest remorse by servile roads,
Dear Sorrow, give me your hand, come with me

Aside. Behold each dead Year bending down
From heaven's balcony in ancient gown;
Watch Regret smiling rise above the wave,

And through an arch the Sun, barely alive,
Seek sleep. Drifting from the East like a grave
Cloth, hear, my love, the gentle Night arrive.

L'OISEAU BLEU
Alphonse Daudet

J'ai dans mon coeur un oiseau bleu,
Une charmante créature
Si mignonne que sa ceinture
N'a pas l'épaisseur d'un cheveu.

Il lui faut du sang pour pâture.
Bien longtemps, je me fis un jeu
De lui donner sa nourriture:
Les petits oiseaux mangent peu.

Mais, sans en rien laisser paraître,
Dans mon coeur il a fait, le traître,
Un trou large comme une main.

Et son bec fin comme une lame,
En continuant son chemin,
M'est entré jusqu'au fond de l'âme! ...

Les Amoureuses.   1863

THE BLUEBIRD

Within my heart there dwells a bird,
A songster of the brightest blue,
The tiniest I ever knew:
His breast a hair would stoutly gird.

On richest blood my bluebird feeds.
For many years I took delight
In giving him his modest needs:
Birds have so small an appetite!

But stealthily the traitor's zeal
Within my heart has made a hole,
A hand in breadth and strangely deep.

His beak, as sharp as tempered steel,
While pecking out his daily keep,
Has reached and pierced my very soul!

ICI-BAS
Sully Prudhomme

Ici-bas tous les lilas meurent,
Tous les chants des oiseaux sont courts.
Je rêve aux étés qui demeurent
    Toujours ...

Ici-bas les lèvres effleurent
Sans rien laisser de leur velours;
Je rêve aux baisers qui demeurent
    Toujours ...

Ici-bas tous les hommes pleurent
Leurs amitiés ou leurs amours;
Je rêve aux couples qui demeurent
    Toujours ...

<u>Stances et poèmes.</u> 1865

HERE BELOW

On earth all lilacs fade too fast,
The songs of birds are brief as day;
I dream of summers that will last
        For aye ...

On earth is lovers' joy soon past,
No kiss its pressure can outstay;
I dream of kisses that will last
        For aye ...

On earth men view with hearts downcast
Their friends and loves of yesterday;
I dream of unions that will last
        For aye ...

LE BRUIT DES CABARETS
Paul Verlaine

Le bruit des cabarets, la fange des trottoirs,
Les platanes déchus s'effeuillant dans l'air noir,
L'omnibus, ouragan de ferraille et de boues,
Qui grince, mal assis entre ses quatre roues,
Et roule ses yeux verts et rouges lentement,
Les ouvriers allant au club, tout en fumant
Leur brûle-gueule au nez des agents de police,
Toits qui dégouttent, murs suintants, pavé qui glisse,
Bitume défoncé, ruisseaux comblant l'égout,
Voilà ma route--avec le paradis au bout.

<u>La Bonne Chanson.</u> 1870

THE NOISE OF CABARETS

The noise of cabarets, the filthy thoroughfare,
The weary plane-trees shedding leaves in the night air,
The bus, a hurricane of iron, mud, and ooze
That sways on its unstable wheels, and creaks, and whose
Red and green eyes from side to side it slowly rolls.
The workmen bound for clubs are flaunting the clay bowls
Of short, mouth-burning pipes beneath the nose of cops.
Slippery cobbles, seeping walls, dripping rooftops,
Bumpy asphalt with drainage that does not suffice,
My customary route--that leads to paradise.

AUBE
Arthur Rimbaud

J'ai embrassé l'aube d'été.

Rien ne bougeait encore au front des palais. L'eau était morte. Les camps d'ombres ne quittaient pas la route du bois. J'ai marché, réveillant les haleines vives et tièdes, et les pierreries regardèrent, et les ailes se levèrent sans bruit.

La première entreprise fut, dans le sentier déjà empli de frais et blêmes éclats, une fleur qui me dit son nom.

Je ris au wasserfall blond qui s'échevela à travers les sapins: à la cime argentée je reconnus la déesse.

Alors je levai un à un les voiles. Dans l'allée, en agitant les bras. Par la plaine, où je l'ai dénoncée au coq. A la grand'ville elle fuyait parmi les clochers et les dômes, et courant comme un mendiant sur les quais de marbre, je la chassais.

En haut de la route, près d'un bois de lauriers, je l'ai entourée avec ses voiles amassés, et j'ai senti un peu son immense corps. L'aube et l'enfant tombèrent au bas du bois.

Au réveil il était midi.

Illuminations. 1886

In "Aube" the feeling of the goodness of nature in the first light of morning is palid (felicity) and unbroken

DAWN

I clasped the summer dawn.

Nothing was stirring yet on the face of the palaces. The water was lifeless. Camps of shadows remained on the forest road. I walked, awakening live warm breaths, and bright gems stared, and wings rose silently.

seems to have mystic powers

The first venture, in a path already filled with cool pale colors, was a flower who told me her name.

I laughed by the blond waterfall that danced wildly through the firs: on the silvery summit I recognized the goddess.

Then I raised the veils one by one. In the wooded lane, by waving my arms. In the open country, where I proclaimed her to the cock. In the city she was taking flight among the bell towers and domes and, running like a beggar on the marble quays, I pursued her.

At the top of the road, near a laurel grove, I embraced her enveloped in veils, and I sensed her immense body. Dawn and child fell on the forest floor.

When I awoke it was noon.

The experience of euphoria through what may be called an epiphany.

attempts to deal w/ a vision

a visionary experience of nature

BRISE MARINE
Stéphane Mallarmé

La chair est triste, hélas! et j'ai lu tous les livres.
Fuir! là-bas fuir! Je sens que les oiseaux sont ivres
D'être parmi l'écume inconnue et les cieux!
Rien, ni les vieux jardins reflétés par les yeux
Ne retiendra ce coeur qui dans la mer se trempe
O nuits! ni la clarté déserte de ma lampe
Sur le vide papier que la blancheur défend
Et ni la jeune femme allaitant son enfant.
Je partirai! Steamer balançant ta mâture,
Lève l'ancre pour une exotique nature!
Un Ennui, désolé par les cruels espoirs,
Croit encore à l'adieu suprême des mouchoirs!
Et peut-être, les mâts, invitant les orages
Sont-ils de ceux qu'un vent penche sur les naufrages
Perdus, sans mâts, sans mâts, ni fertiles îlots ...
Mais, O mon coeur, entends le chant des matelots!

Poésies. 1887 et 1889

SEA BREEZE

The flesh is sad, alas! and I've read every book.
Escape! flee afar! I feel that the wild birds brook
No bounds of joy in foreign spray, in stranger skies!
Nothing, not ancient gardens reflected in eyes,
Shall hold this heart that's tempered in the great sea's might,
O nights! not even my abandoned lamp's pale light
On empty paper waiting white and undefiled,
And not the young wife who is suckling her small child.
I will depart! O ship, that cants as tall masts sway,
For strange exotic countries now your anchor weigh!
My poor bored dreary heart, laid waste by hopes untrue,
Can still respond when kerchiefs wave a last adieu!
Perhaps these masts will court the storms, inviting gales,
Will someday lean across a wreck that's lost, no sails,
No masts, no fertile isle in sight, drifting along ...
But harken, O my heart, and hear the sailors' song!

UNE JEUNE FILLE PARLE
Jean Moréas

Les fenouils m'ont dit: Il t'aime si
Follement qu'il est à ta merci;
Pour son revenir va t'apprêter.
--Les fenouils ne savent que flatter!
Dieu ait pitié de mon âme.

Les pâquerettes m'ont dit: Pourquoi
Avoir remis ta foi dans sa foi?
Son coeur est tanné comme un soudard.
--Pâquerettes, vous parlez trop tard!
Dieu ait pitié de mon âme.

Les sauges m'ont dit: Ne l'attends pas,
Il s'est endormi dans d'autres bras.
--O sauges, tristes sauges, je veux
Vous tresser toutes dans mes cheveux ...
Dieu ait pitié de mon âme.

Le Pèlerin passionné. 1891

A GIRL SPEAKS

The fennels said to me: Love's thrall
Has placed him at your beck and call;
Go deck yourself for him to see.
--What flatterers the fennels be!
God have mercy on my soul.

The Easter daisies said forsooth:
Why trust your fate to that man's truth?
His heart is worn by old loves' weight.
--Good daisies, your advice is late!
God have mercy on my soul.

The gray-green sages said: Don't bide;
He's sleeping at another's side.
--O sad, sad sages, my despair
Now bids me twine you in my hair ...
God have mercy on my soul.

CHAQUE HEURE OU JE SONGE
Emile Verhaeren

Chaque heure où je songe à ta bonté
Si simplement profonde,
Je me confonds en prières vers toi.

Je suis venu si tard
Vers la douceur de ton regard,
Et de si loin vers tes deux mains tendues,
Tranquillement, par à travers les étendues !

J'avais en moi tant de rouille tenace
Qui me rongeait, à dents rapaces,
La confiance.

J'étais si lourd, j'étais si las,
J'étais si vieux de méfiance,
J'étais si lourd, j'étais si las
Du vain chemin de tous mes pas.

Je méritais si peu la merveilleuse joie
De voir tes pieds illuminer ma voie,
Que j'en reste tremblant encore et presque en pleurs
Et humble, à tout jamais, en face du bonheur.

<u>Les Heures claires.</u>   1896

AS I MUSE EACH HOUR

As I muse each hour on your dear heart's love,
So simple and profound,
I lose myself in gratitude to you.

So late, so late I drew
Into the radiance of your eyes,
And from so far, so far, toward your dear hands
Stretched tranquilly to me across the lands.

I had in me so much deep-eaten rust
That gnawed with greedy fangs my trust,
My confidence.

I was so heartsick and weary,
I was so old in mistrust,
I was so heartsick and weary
Of plodding on in futile dust.

So little I earned the wondrous delight
Of seeing your steps illumine my night,
That I stand trembling still and almost weep,
Forever humbled by a joy so deep.

LES HEURES CLAIRES XXIX
Emile Verhaeren

Vous m'avez dit, tel soir, des paroles si belles
Que sans doute les fleurs, qui se penchaient vers nous,
Soudain nous ont aimés et que l'une d'entre elles,
Pour nous toucher tous deux, tomba sur nos genoux.

Vous me parliez des temps prochains où nos années,
Comme des fruits trop mûrs, se laisseraient cueillir;
Comment éclaterait le glas des destinées,
Et comme on s'aimerait, en se sentant vieillir.

Votre voix m'enlaçait comme une chère étreinte,
Et votre coeur brûlait si tranquillement beau
Qu'en ce moment j'aurais pu voir s'ouvrir sans crainte
Les tortueux chemins qui vont vers le tombeau.

Les Heures claires. 1896

SHINING HOURS

In the garden at twilight one evening you spoke
Words so sweet that the flowers that bent down to hear
Were all suddenly touched by a love so sincere,
And a blossom in sympathy fell on our knees.

You were talking to me of the time drawing near
When our years, like ripe fruit, would be ready to fall;
Of the peal of the bell that would toll our recall,
Of the strength of our love as we came to old age.

Your dear voice was enfolding me like an embrace,
And your heart was so loving, so fervently chaste,
At that moment, in fearless content, I had faced
The most perilous paths that lead down to the grave.

CHANSON
Maurice Maeterlinck

Et s'il revenait un jour
    Que faut-il lui dire?
--Dites-lui qu'on l'attendit
    Jusqu'à s'en mourir ...

Et s'il m'interroge encore
    Sans me reconnaître?
--Parlez-lui comme une soeur.
    Il souffre peut-être ...

Et s'il veut savoir pourquoi
    La salle est déserte?
--Montrez-lui la lampe éteinte
    Et la porte ouverte ...

Et s'il m'interroge encore
    Sur la dernière heure?
--Dites-lui que j'ai souri
    De peur qu'il ne pleure ...

<u>Douze (Quinze) Chansons.</u> 1896

SONG

"And if he should come back some day
    What must I say to him?"
"Say that I watched for his return
    Until my eyes grew dim."

"And if he asks me other things
    Without recalling me?"
"Speak softly, gently, to him then.
    He may need sympathy ..."

"And if he might perhaps ask why
    The house is gay no more?"
"Show him the lamp extinguished now
    And show the open door ..."

"And if he should inquire about
    The final agony?"
"Remember, please, to say I smiled
    Lest he might weep for me ..."

CETTE FILLE, ELLE EST MORTE
Paul Fort

Cette fille, elle est morte, est morte dans ses amours.
Ils l'ont portée en terre, en terre au point du jour.
Ils l'ont couchée toute seule, toute seule en ses atours.
Ils l'ont couchée toute seule, toute seule en son cercueil.
Ils sont rev'nus gaîment, gaîment avec le jour.
Ils ont chanté gaîment, gaîment: "Chacun son tour.
Cette fille, elle est morte, est morte dans ses amours."
Ils sont allés aux champs, aux champs comme tous les jours...

Ballades françaises, Vol. I. 1896

BALLAD OF A DEAD GIRL

The merry lass is dead, is dead in a love-bed.
They put her in the earth, in earth at dawn of day.
They laid her all alone, dressed for a gala-day.
They laid her all alone, weighed down by coffin lead.
They came back gaily, gaily at break of day.
They sang gaily, gaily: "Everyone must pay.
The merry lass is dead, is dead in a love-bed."
They went to work in fields, as any other day ...

ODELETTE I
Henri de Régnier

Un petit roseau m'a suffi
Pour faire frémir l'herbe haute
Et tout le pré
Et les doux saules
Et le ruisseau qui chante aussi;
Un petit roseau m'a suffi
A faire chanter la forêt.

Ceux qui passent l'ont entendu
Au fond du soir, en leurs pensées,
Dans le silence et dans le vent,
Clair ou perdu,
Proche ou lointain ...
Ceux qui passent en leurs pensées
En écoutant, au fond d'eux-mêmes,
L'entendront encore et l'entendent
Toujours qui chante.

Il m'a suffi
De ce petit roseau cueilli
A la fontaine où vint l'Amour
Mirer, un jour,
Sa face grave
Et qui pleurait,
Pour faire pleurer ceux qui passent
Et trembler l'herbe et frémir l'eau:
Et j'ai, du souffle d'un roseau,
Fait chanter toute la forêt.

<u>Les Jeux rustiques et divins.</u>   1897

ODELETTE I

One little reed has sufficed me
To set high grasses quivering
And all the plain
And willows sweet
And the stream that sings to the sea;
One little reed has sufficed me
To wake the mighty forest's strain.

Those who pass have heard it oft
At evening's close, in their own thoughts,
In the still air and in the wind,
Loud-voiced or soft,
Near or remote ...
Those who pass in their own thoughts
While listening, deep within their mind
Will hear again nor fail to find
Eternal song.

It sufficed me
This little reed that I pulled free
Close by the fountain where came Love
To pose above,
Gravely one day
And sorrowing,
To make the passersby lament
And wildly thrill the stream and mead;
And with the breath of one small reed,
I have made all the forest sing.

ODELETTE IV
Henri de Régnier

Si j'ai parlé
De mon amour, c'est à l'eau lente
Qui m'écoute quand je me penche
Sur elle; si j'ai parlé
De mon amour, c'est au vent
Qui rit et chuchote entre les branches;
Si j'ai parlé de mon amour, c'est à l'oiseau
Qui passe et chante
Avec le vent;
Si j'ai parlé
C'est à l'écho.

Si j'ai aimé de grand amour,
Triste ou joyeux,
Ce sont tes yeux;
Si j'ai aimé de grand amour,
Ce fut ta bouche grave et douce,
Ce fut ta bouche;
Si j'ai aimé de grand amour,
Ce furent ta chair tiède et tes mains fraîches.
Et c'est ton ombre que je cherche.

Les Jeux rustiques et divins. 1897

ODELETTE IV

If I have spoken
Of my love, 'twas to slow springs
That mirror-like received my vows
And sighs; if I have spoken
Of my love, 'twas to the wind
That laughs and whispers in the boughs;
If I have spoken of my love, 'twas to the bird
That roving sings
With the soft wind;
What I have said,
The echoes heard.

If I have loved with lasting love,
In smiles or sighs,
It was your eyes;
If I have loved with lasting love,
It was your lips so sweetly grave,
It was your lips;
If I have loved with lasting love,
'Twas your warm flesh and your cool hands.
And now it is your shade I seek.

ODELETTE XI
Henri de Régnier

Chante si doucement que j'entends
A travers ta voix d'autres voix,
Sa tendresse sera plus tendre
Si tu cueilles en une branche
Le murmure de tout le bois.

Ecoute, cette vague m'apporte
L'écho lointain de toute la mer,
Et sa rumeur profonde et forte
Déferle toute en ce bruit clair;

Ton pas, sur le seuil de ma porte
Sandales d'or, talon de fer,
--Que la corbeille que tu portes
Soit de jonc ou d'osier vert,
Pleine de fleurs ou de feuilles mortes--
Ton pas sur le seuil de ma porte
C'est la Vie et toute la Vie
Qui entre et marche dans ma vie,
Sandale souple ou talon lourd,
Douce ou farouche,
Et le baiser nu de sa bouche
Est tout l'Amour.

<u>Les Jeux rustiques et divins.</u> 1897

ODELETTE XI

Sing so softly that I hear
Other voices as you sing;
Your dear tones will be more dear
If you gather in one spray
All the woods' deep murmuring.

Then listen as this wave brings me
The far-off echo of the sea,
And its great long thundering roar
Is heard when one wave breaks on shore.

Your step on the sill of my door,
Heel of iron, sandals of gold,
--Whether the basket that you hold
Of willow wands or rushes made,
With flowers filled or with dead leaves--
Your step on the sill of my door,
Is Life with its infinite wealth
That enters and walks in my life,
Supple sandal or heavy heel,
Gentle or rude,
And its kiss, the kiss of your lips,
Is Love renewed.

ELEGIE DOUBLE
Henri de Régnier

Ami, le hibou pleure où venait la colombe,
Et ton sang souterrain a fleuri sur ta tombe,
Et mes yeux qui t'ont vu sont las d'avoir pleuré
L'inexorable absence où tu t'es retiré
Loin de mes bras pieux et de ma bouche triste.
Reviens! le doux jardin mystérieux t'invite
Et ton pas sera doux à sa mélancolie;
Tu viendras, les pieds nus et la face vieillie,
Peut-être, car la route est longue qui ramène
De la rive du Styx à notre humble fontaine
Qui pleure goutte à goutte et rit d'avoir pleuré.

Ta maison te regarde, ami! J'ai préparé
Sur le plateau d'argent, sur le plateau d'ébène
La coupe de cristal et la coupe de frêne,
Les figues et le vin, le lait et les olives,
Et j'ai huilé les gonds de la porte d'une huile
Qui la fera s'ouvrir ainsi que pour une ombre;
Mais je prendrai la lampe et par l'escalier sombre
Nous monterons tous deux en nous tenant la main;
Puis, dans la chambre vaste où le songe divin
T'a ramené des bords du royaume oublieux,
Nous nous tiendrons debout, face à face, joyeux
De l'étrange douceur de rejoindre nos lèvres,
O voyageur venu des roseaux de la grève
Que ne réveille pas l'aurore ni le vent!
Je t'ai tant aimé mort que tu seras vivant

DOUBLE ELEGY

My dear, the owl cries where the dove used to come,
And your earth-hidden blood has enflowered your grave,
And my eyes that beheld you are worn with lamenting
The silence unyielding where you have withdrawn,
Remote from my arms and from my sad lips far.
Come back! The garden's sweet mystery invites you
And your step will be kind in its melancholy;
You will come, your feet bare, and your face grown old,
It may be, for long is the road that returns
From the bank of the Styx to our humble fountain,
That weeps drop by drop and laughs at its weeping.

Your house watches for you, my dear! I've prepared
On the pure silver tray, on the ebony tray,
The goblet of crystal, the goblet of ash,
The figs and the wine, the milk and the olives,
And I've oiled the door's hinges with oil of a sort
That will make it swing open as though for a ghost;
But I'll take the lamp and by the dark staircase
We'll mount hand in hand, just we two alone;
Then in the vast room where the vision divine
Called you back from the kingdom of Lethe,
We shall stand face to face, lost in joy
At the sweet renewed strangeness of mingling our lips,
O traveller returned from the reeds of the strand
Whom neither the dawn nor the wind can awaken!
I've loved you so dearly that you'll live again

Et j'aurai soin, n'ayant plus d'espoir ni d'attente,
De vider la clepsydre et d'éteindre la lampe.

--Laisse brûler la lampe et pleurer la clepsydre
Car le jardin autour de notre maison vide
Se fleurira de jeunes fleurs sans que reviennent
Mes lèvres pour reboire encore à la fontaine;
Les baisers pour jamais meurent avec les bouches.
Laisse la figue mûre et les olives rousses;
Hélas! les fruits sont bons aux lèvres qui sont chair.
Mais j'habite un royaume au delà de la Mer
Ténébreuse, et mon corps est cendre sous le marbre.
Je suis une Ombre, et si mon pas lent se hasarde
Au jardin d'autrefois et dans la maison noire
Où tu m'attends du fond de toute ta mémoire,
Tes chers bras ne pourront étreindre mon fantôme;
Tu pleurerais le souvenir de ma chair d'homme,
A moins que dans ton âme anxieuse et fidèle
Tu m'attendes en rêve à la porte éternelle,
Me regardant venir à travers la nuit sombre,
Et que ton pur amour soit digne de mon ombre.

<u>Les Jeux rustiques et divins.</u>   1897

And I shall take care, my long vigil ended,
To drain the clepsydra and extinguish the lamp.

--Let the lamp shine and the clepsydra weep,
For the garden surrounding our empty abode
Will blossom in springtime again ere my lips
Come back to drink one more time at the fountain;
A kiss will die with the lips of a lover.
Let the figs ripen and the olives grow black;
Alas! Fruit is good in the mouth of the living.
But I dwell in a kingdom beyond the dark Sea,
And my body is ashes under the marble.
I am a Shade, and if my slow step venture
In yesterday's garden and in the dark house
Where you wait for me in the depths of your memory,
Your dear arms may never encompass my shadow;
You would weep in remembrance of my earthly frame,
Unless in your anguished and faithful soul,
You await me in dreams at eternity's portal,
Watching me traverse the night's gloomy shadows,
And may your pure love match the love of my spirit.

POUR LA PORTE DES EXILES
Henri de Régnier

Puisque j'ai vu crouler sous la pioche et la hache,
Ma maison vide, au moins que l'herbe haute cache
Sa ruine à jamais et son triste décombre.
De l'homme que j'étais je suis devenu l'ombre,
Et l'injuste Colère et la mauvaise Haine
Me montrent l'âpre exil et la route lointaine
Du double doigt tendu de leurs deux mains crispées,
Et puisqu'on m'interdit la balance et l'épée,
Je prends le bâton noir et la sandale blanche;
Qu'on ne vienne jamais me tirer par la manche
Ou par le pan usé de mon manteau d'exil.
Dieux cléments, détournez le mal et le péril
De l'ingrate cité qui me mord au jarret!
La ville ne vaut pas la mer et la forêt;
Et, proscrit vagabond que le vent déracine,
J'aurai l'aube charmante et l'aurore divine
Qui me consoleront de l'ombre où je m'en vais;
Et, si le sort s'acharne à mon destin mauvais,
Je pourrai, pour ma bouche amère, sèche et lasse
De cette solitude où mon pas se harasse,
Cueillir, sans peur, un soir, la jusquiame velue,
La noire belladone ou la verte ciguë.

<u>Les Jeux rustiques et divins.</u> 1897

FOR THE GATE OF EXILES

Since I've seen my home razed by the axe and the spade,
It remains but to pray that tall grasses may shade
Its forsaken debris with an emerald screen.
I am only the mask of the man I have been,
While unjustified Anger and menacing Hate
Point the far road for me and the sad exile's fate
With the fingers of scorn that enforce their decree.
And since both the scales and the sword are denied me,
The white sandal I'll take and the pilgrim's black cane;
Let no man importune me or seek to detain
Me by plucking my cloak or by touching my arm.
Turn aside, O compassionate gods, every harm
From the town whose ingratitude ever must hound me!
Can the city surpass the free woods and the sea?
Even though my abode fickle winds now assign,
I shall have the pearl dawn and the sunrise divine
To console my long sojourn beyond the dark sea;
And if fate should chastise me too mercilessly,
I shall gather, some evening, with no inward cry
For my lips that are bitter and weary and dry
From the solitude drear that the harsh fates ordain
Belladonna, green hemlock, or hairy henbane.

VOEU / Henri de Régnier

Je voudrais pour tes yeux la plaine
Et une forêt verte et rousse,
Lointaine
Et douce
A l'horizon sous un ciel clair,
Ou des collines
Aux belles lignes
Flexibles et lentes et vaporeuses
Et qui sembleraient fondre en la douceur de l'air,
Ou des collines,
Ou la forêt ...

Je voudrais
Que tu entendes,
Forte, vaste, profonde et tendre,
La grande voix sourde de la mer
Qui se lamente
Comme l'Amour;
Et, par instants, tout près de toi,
Dans l'intervalle,
Que tu entendes,
Tout près de toi,
Une colombe
Dans le silence,
Et faible et douce
Comme l'Amour,
Un peu dans l'ombre,
Que tu entendes
Sourdre une source ...

Je voudrais des fleurs pour tes mains,
Et pour tes pas
Un petit sentier d'herbe et de sable
Qui monte un peu et qui descende
Et tourne et semble
S'en aller au fond du silence,
Un tout petit sentier de sable
Où marqueraient un peu tes pas,
Nos pas,
Ensemble!

<u>Les Médailles d'argile</u>.   1900

WISH

For your eyes I wish a plain
And forest green and golden-red
Far off
And soft,
On an azure horizon spread.
Or maybe hills
With lovely lines
That are vaporous, flowing, slow,
And that seem to dissolve in the langorous air,
Either these hills,
Or the forest ...

For your ears
To hear, I wish
The thundering voice of the sea
That is deep and tender and strong
And makes, like Love,
A long lament;
And sometimes close to you I hope
That you will hear
Between the waves,
Quite close to you,
A cooing dove
In the sea's lull,
Fragile and faint
And sweet, like Love,
Or that you hear
In quiet shade
A purling spring ...

I wish flowers for your hands,
And for your feet
A little path all sand and grass
That climbs a knoll and then goes down
And bends and seems
To lose itself in silent depths,
A tiny little path of sand
On which your feet would leave their print,
Our prints,
We two.

CHANSON
Henri de Régnier

Que me fait toute la terre
Inutile où tu n'as pas
En marchant marqué tes pas
Sur le sable ou la poussière!

Il n'est de fleuve attendu
Par ma soif qui s'y étanche
Que l'eau qui sourd et s'épanche
De la source où tu as bu;

La seule fleur qui m'attire
Est celle où je trouverai
Le souvenir empourpré
De ta bouche et de ton rire;

Et, sous la courbe des cieux,
La mer pour moi n'est immense
Que parce qu'elle commence
A la couleur de tes yeux.

<u>La Sandale ailée</u>. 1906

SONG

What is all the world to me?
What to me are foreign lands,
If impressed in dust or sands
Your small print I fail to see?

What is water to my thirst?
What the clearest rill that flows
Sparkling down from mountain snows,
If you have not drunk there first?

Oh, what flower can eclipse
Eglantine that's budded new,
And recalls the rosy hue
Of your laughter and your lips?

And beneath the curving skies
The great sea is only vast
When its rippling wave is cast
With the color of your eyes!

LA VOIX
Henri de Régnier

Je ne veux de personne auprès de ma tristesse
Ni même ton cher pas et ton visage aimé,
Ni ta main indolente et qui d'un doigt caresse
Le ruban paresseux et le livre fermé.

Laissez-moi. Que ma porte aujourd'hui reste close;
N'ouvrez pas ma fenêtre au vent frais du matin;
Mon coeur est aujourd'hui misérable et morose
Et tout me paraît sombre et tout me semble vain.

Ma tristesse me vient de plus loin que moi-même,
Elle m'est étrangère et ne m'appartient pas,
Et tout homme, qu'il chante ou qu'il rie ou qu'il aime,
A son heure l'entend qui lui parle tout bas,

Et quelque chose alors se remue et s'éveille,
S'agite, se répand et se lamente en lui,
A cette sourde voix qui lui dit à l'oreille
Que la fleur de la vie est cendre dans son fruit.

<u>La Sandale ailée</u>. 1906

THE VOICE

I want nobody near to disturb my sad mood;
I don't want your dear step and affectionate look,
Nor your indolent hands whose slow motions intrude
As they finger the ribbon that marks a closed book.

Leave me now. Let my door for the day remain closed;
Let my casement be shut to the morning's cool air;
For to gloom and dejection my soul is disposed,
I see darkness and vanity now everywhere.

My morose frame of mind comes from elsewhere than me;
It is stranger to me and no mood-wave of mine.
Though he sing, though he laugh, though his heart's love he see,
Every man in his time hears the low-whispered sign;

And then something in him is awakened and stirs,
And a grievous lament overpowers his trust
When this treacherous voice in his ear first avers
That the flower of life in its fruit is but dust.

NOEL SCEPTIQUE
Jules Laforgue

Noël! Noël? j'entends les cloches dans la nuit ...
Et j'ai, sur ces feuillets sans foi, posé ma plume:
O souvenirs, chantez! tout mon orgueil s'enfuit,
Et je me sens repris de ma grande amertume.

Ah! ces voix dans la nuit chantant Noël! Noël!
M'apportent de la nef qui, là-bas, s'illumine,
Un si tendre, un si doux reproche maternel
Que mon coeur trop gonflé crève dans ma poitrine ...

Et j'écoute longtemps les cloches dans la nuit ...
Je suis le paria de la famille humaine,
A qui le vent apporte en un sale réduit
La poignante rumeur d'une fête lointaine.

<u>Le Sanglot de la terre.</u> 1901

NOEL SCEPTIQUE

Noël! Noël? I hear the midnight bells
And pose my pen above this worldly page.
Sing, memories! my erstwhile pride has turned
To bitterness that nothing can assuage.

Those happy voices ringing out Noël
From that new-lighted nave in the still night
Come freighted with a mother's sweet reproach
That breaks my heart already swollen tight.

And long I listen to the midnight bells ...
Alone, a human outcast, desolate,
To whom the wind in this vile hovel brings
The poignant murmur of a distant fête.

le porche du mystère de la deuxième vertu [extrait]
Charles Péguy

O belle nuit, nuit au grand manteau, ma fille au manteau
 étoilé
Tu me rappelles, à moi-même tu me rappelles ce grand
 silence qu'il y avait
Avant que j'eusse ouvert les écluses d'ingratitude.
Et tu m'annonces, à moi-même tu m'annonces ce grand
 silence qu'il y aura
Quand je les aurai fermées.
O douce, ô grande, ô sainte, ô belle nuit, peut-être la plus
 sainte de mes filles, nuit à la grande robe, à la
 robe étoilée
Tu me rappelles ce grand silence qu'il y avait dans le monde
Avant le commencement du règne de l'homme.
Tu m'annonces ce grand silence qu'il y aura
Après la fin du règne de l'homme, quand j'aurai repris mon
 sceptre.
Et j'y pense quelque fois d'avance, car cet homme fait
 vraiment beaucoup de bruit.
Mais surtout, Nuit, tu me rappelles cette nuit.
Et je me la rappellerai éternellement.
La neuvième heure avait sonné. C'était dans le pays de
 mon peuple d'Israël.
Tout était consommé. Cette énorme aventure.
Depuis la sixième heure il y avait eu des ténèbres sur tout
 le pays, jusqu'à la neuvième heure.
Tout était consommé. Ne parlons plus de cela. Ca me
 fait mal.
Cette incroyable descente de mon fils parmi les hommes.
Chez les hommes.
Pour ce qu'ils en ont fait.
Ces trente ans qu'il fut charpentier chez les hommes
Ces trois ans qu'il fut une sorte de prédicateur chez les
 hommes.
Un prêtre.
Ces trois jours où il fut une victime chez les hommes.
Parmi les hommes.
Ces trois nuits où il fut un mort chez les hommes.
Parmi les hommes morts.
Ces siècles et ces siècles où il est une hostie chez les
 hommes.
Tout était consommé, cette incroyable aventure
Par laquelle, moi, Dieu, j'ai les bras liés pour mon éternité.
Cette aventure par laquelle mon Fils m'a lié les bras.

THE PORTICO OF THE MYSTERY
OF THE SECOND VIRTUE (extract)

O beautiful night, night of the great mantle, my daughter of
        the starry mantle
You remind me, even me, of the great silence there was
Before I had opened the flood-gates of ingratitude.
And you presage for me, even for me, the great silence
        there will be
When I have closed them.
O sweet, O great, O holy; O beautiful night, perhaps the
        holiest of my daughters, night of the great robe,
        of the starry robe
You remind me of the great silence there was in the world
Before the beginning of the reign of man.
You presage for me the great silence there will be
At the end of the reign of man, when I have resumed my
        scepter.
And I look forward to it sometimes, for truly man makes a
        lot of noise.
But especially, O Night, you remind me of that night,
And I shall remember it forever.
The ninth hour had struck in the country of my people
        Israel.
It was all over. That tremendous adventure.
From the sixth hour there had been darkness over all the
        land until the ninth hour.
It was all over. Let us not talk of that any more. It pains
        me.
That unbelievable descent of my son among men.
Into the midst of men,
When you think how they reacted.
Those thirty years that he was a carpenter in the midst of men
Those three years that he was a sort of preacher in the
        midst of men.
A priest.
Those three days that he was a victim in the midst of men.
Among men.
Those three nights that he was a corpse in the midst of men.
Among dead men.
Those centuries and centuries that he has been a host in the
        midst of men.
It was all over, the unbelievable adventure
That has tied my hands for all eternity.
The adventure by which my Son has tied my hands.

Pour éternellement liant les bras de ma justice, pour
        éternellement déliant les bras de ma miséricorde.
Et contre ma justice inventant une justice même.
Une justice d'amour.   Une justice d'Espérance.   Tout était
        consommé.
Ce qu'il fallait.   Comme il avait fallu.   Comme mes prophè-
        tes l'avaient annoncé.   Le voile du temple s'était
        déchiré en deux, depuis le haut jusqu'en bas.
La terre avait tremblé; des rocher s'étaient fendus.
Des sépulcres s'étaient ouverts, et plusieurs corps des
        saints qui étaient morts étaient ressuscités.
Et environ la neuvième heure mon Fils avait poussé
Le cri qui ne s'effacera point.   Tout était consommé.
        Les soldats s'en étaient retournés dans leurs
        casernes.
Riant et plaisantant parce que c'était un service de fini.
Un tour de garde qu'ils ne prendraient plus.
Seul un centenier demeurait, et quelques hommes
Un tout petit poste pour garder ce gibet sans importance.
La potence où mon Fils pendait.
Seules quelques femmes étaient demeurées.
La Mère était là.
Et peut-être aussi quelques disciples, et encore on n'en est
        pas bien sûr.
Or tout homme a le droit d'ensevelir son fils
Tout homme sur terre, s'il a ce grand malheur
De ne pas être mort avant son fils.   Et moi seul, moi Dieu,
Les bras liés par cette aventure,
Moi seul à cette minute père après tant de pères,
Moi seul je ne pouvais pas ensevelir mon fils.
C'est alors, ô nuit, que tu vins.
O ma fille chère entre toutes et je le vois encore et je
        verrai cela dans mon éternité
C'est alors ô Nuit que tu vins et dans un grand linceul tu
        ensevelis
Le Centenier et ses hommes romains,
La Vierge et les saintes femmes,
Et cette montagne et cette vallée, sur qui le soir
        descendait,
Et mon peuple d'Israël et les pécheurs et ensemble celui
        qui mourait, qui était mort pour eux
Et les hommes de Joseph d'Arimathé qui déjà s'approchaient
Portant le linceul blanc.

1911

Eternally tying the hands of my justice, eternally loosing
    the hands of my mercy.
And even inventing a justice opposed to my justice.
A justice of love. A justice of Hope. It was all over.
That which was necessary. As it had to be. As my
    prophets had foretold it. The veil of the temple
    had been rent in twain, from top to bottom.
The earth had quaked; rocks had split.
Graves had opened, and several bodies of saints who were
    dead were restored to life.
And about the ninth hour my Son had uttered
The cry that will never fade. It was all over. The
    soldiers had returned to their barracks.
Laughing and joking because another task was finished.
One more guard duty they would not have to stand.
Only one centurion remained, and a few men
A very small guard for the unimportant gibbet
The gallows where my Son was hanging.
Only a few women had remained.
The Mother was there.
And maybe also a few disciples, that is not certain.
Now every man has the right to bury his son
Every man on earth, if he has the great misfortune
Not to die before his son. And I alone, God,
My hands tied by this adventure,
I, alone, a father at that moment after so many fathers,
I alone was unable to bury my son.
It was then, O night, that you came.
O my daughter dearest of all and I see him still and I shall
    see that throughout eternity
It was then O Night that you came and in a great shroud
    you enveloped
The centurion and his Roman men,
The Virgin and the holy women,
And that mountain and that valley, where the dusk was draw-
    ing in,
And my people Israel and the sinners, along with him who
    was dying, who had died for them
And the servants of Joseph of Arimathea who were already
    approaching,
Bearing the white grave-cloth.

LE PONT MIRABEAU
Guillaume Apollinaire

Sous le pont Mirabeau coule la Seine
    Et nos amours
   Faut-il qu'il m'en souvienne
La joie venait toujours après la peine

  Vienne la nuit sonne l'heure
  Les jours s'en vont je demeure

Les mains dans les mains restons face à face
    Tandis que sous
   Le pont de nos bras passe
Des éternels regards l'onde si lasse

  Vienne la nuit sonne l'heure
  Les jours s'en vont je demeure

L'amour s'en va comme cette eau courante
    L'amour s'en va
   Comme la vie est lente
Et comme l'espérance est violente

  Vienne la nuit sonne l'heure
  Les jours s'en vont je demeure

Passent les jours et passent les semaines
    Ni temps passé
   Ni les amours reviennent
Sous le pont Mirabeau coule la Seine

  Vienne la nuit sonne l'heure
  Les jours s'en vont je demeure

<u>Alcools</u>.   1913

MIRABEAU BRIDGE

The Seine flows on beneath the Mirabeau
              Along with love
           Must I remember though
Joy follows sorrow it was always so

    Let hours strike night come again
    The days go by I remain

Your hands in mine let us stand face to face
            While underneath
             Our bridge of arms waves trace
A path grown weary of our staring race

    Let hours strike night come again
    The days go by I remain

And love passes by like this flowing stream
            Love passes by
           How dreary our lives seem
And hope is always a violent dream

    Let hours strike night come again
    The days go by I remain

Days come to an end and the weeks too go
            No time returns
          Nor do our loves twice glow
The Seine flows on beneath the Mirabeau

    Let hours strike night come again
    The days go by I remain

BASCULE
Pierre Reverdy

La lutte du vent dans le port
    Les mots brouillés dans l'air
Que la vague pousse plus fort
    En dessous quelque chose passe
On attend que tout se défasse
L'eau monte par-dessus
    Les pierres disparaissent
Et de l'autre côté il y a des jours qui naissent
Les jours luisants amoncelés
  Au bord de l'horizon qui les laisse tomber
    Un à un
La main qui guide les saisons se trompe
Et moi je tombe
    Ma raison
      glisse
Entre les lames sous le pont
Je vois l'autre côté du monde

<u>Sources du vent.</u> 1929

SEESAW

The struggle of wind in the port
              Fractured words in the air
That waves catch and distort
              The motion below increases
Everything may fall to pieces
The water climbs above
              Stones slip beneath the tide
And there are days awaiting birth on the other side
Sparkling days built in a crown
    On the rim of the horizon that lets them drop down
             One by one
The hand that directs the seasons is wrong
I am falling
              My reason
                  drifts
Among the waves under the bridge
I see the other side of the world

LE TEMPS D'UN ECLAIR
Paul Eluard

Elle n'est pas là.

La femme au tablier guette la pluie aux vitres
En spectacle tous les nuages jouent au plus fin
Une fillette de peu de poids
Passée au bleu
Joue sur un canapé crevé
Le silence a des remords.

J'ai suivi les murs d'un rue très longue
Des pierres des pavés des verdures
De la terre de la neige du sable
Des ombres du soleil de l'eau
Vie apparente

Sans oublier qu'elle était là
A promener un grand jardin
A becqueter un mûrier blanc
La neige de ses rires stérilisait la boue
Sa démarche était vierge.

<u>La Vie immédiate.</u> 1932

IN A FLASH

She is not there.

The aproned woman watches raindrops on the pane
The clouds are all playfully racing each other
A little girl of small importance
In blue ignored
Is playing on a brokendown couch
The silence is remorseful.

I followed the walls of a long long street
Over rocks over paving stones over grass
Then earth then snow then sand
Shadows sunshine and water
Apparent life

Without forgetting that she was there
Walking a vast garden
Pecking a white mulberry tree
The snow of her laughter sterilized the mud
Her bearing was virginal.

PSAUME XLI
Patrice de La Tour du Pin

Pourquoi m'avoir donné tant de grâces, Seigneur?--il faudra
    bien que j'en réponde.
Vous m'avez débordé d'indulgence,--je n'ai pas ma part de
    tristesse.
Je suis bien trop faible pour vous la réclamer,--faut-il
    vraiment qu'il y ait des êtres de bonheur?
Je me sens plus proche de Vous dans le bonheur que dans le
    renoncement,--Seigneur, ayez pitié si je le garde pur.
Je n'ai pas mérité de tels privilèges terrestres,--mais j'ai
    reconnu chaque fois votre don.
J'ai l'angoisse d'être trop heureux au milieu des misérables,--
    je le confesse même si cela doit scandaliser.
Que l'on me dise: il ne veut pas prendre part!--que l'on
    me jette: il s'enterre en lui pour ne pas souffrir!
Mais je ne peux pas faire que ma joie soit obscure!--je ne
    peux pas faire que ma joie ne soit pas Vous!

<u>Les Psaumes.</u> 1938

PSALM XLI

Why have You given me so many blessings, Lord?--I shall
    be held accountable for them.
You have overwhelmed me with kindness--I do not have my
    share of sadness.
I am much too weak to beseech You for it--must there truly
    be some people at peace?
I feel closer to You in happiness than in sacrifice,--Lord,
    be merciful if I keep it pure.
I have not deserved such favors on earth,--but each time I
    have known it was Your gift.
It hurts me to be too happy in the midst of the wretched,--
    I confess this even if it gives offence.
Let them say: he is unwilling to participate!--let them cast up
    to me: he withdraws into himself so as not to suffer.
But I cannot force my joy to be dim!--I cannot force my joy
    not to be You!

CANTO XXV
Pierre Emmanuel

O divine ironie
Visage entre tous mes visages
j'ai tant prié
j'ai tant scruté mon âme
à te chercher
que mes yeux las se sont changés
en larmes

Je sais maintenant
ô seul Visage
qu'il faut briser la roue sauvage
de ce présent toujours absent
mon âme,
pour te trouver en cette nuit sans âge
où tu m'attends

<u>XX Cantos.</u> 1942

CANTO XXV

O divine irony
Face among all my faces
I've prayed so long
I've scanned my soul so long
seeking you
that my tired eyes have changed
to tears

And now I know
O Face unique
that I must break the untamed wheel
of this ever absent present
my soul,
if I would find you in that timeless night
where you await me

LE LILAS BLANC
Mathilde Monnier

Mon âme a capté la fragrance
d'un grappe de lilas,
de lilas blanc
penché sur mon enfance.

Mon âme est à jamais captive
d'une branche de lilas
d'une branche fugitive
de lilas blanc.

<u>Dispersion</u>. 1942

THE WHITE LILAC

My soul has kept the fragrant scent
of a lilac branch,
of a lilac white
above my childhood bent.

My soul is still a captive tight
of a lilac branch
of a lilac white
of a vanishing branch of white.

LE ROSSIGNOL
Mathilde Monnier

Le rossignol a chanté
sur un cyprès de lune baigné.

La voix entendue,
continue
à travers le profond lointain,
continue de chanter
à travers les années
dans tous les jardins
de lune baignés.

<u>Dispersion</u>.   1942

THE NIGHTINGALE

A nightingale has sung its tune
on a cypress tree bathed by the moon.

The sound of the song
echoes along
through ultimate far-away lands
continues its tune
through years unborn
in all of the gardens
bathed by the moon.

LE CHANT DU COQ
Mathilde Monnier

Le chant du coq déchire le silence.
Une voix lui répond.
Un autre appel ...
Des voix de plus en plus lointaines
crient dans la nuit dense.

Qui m'appelle ?
Qui me répond ?

<u>Dispersion</u>. 1942

COCKCROW

A cock's crow tears the silent night.
A second cock replies.
Another calls ...
Then voices far and farther off
Still other cries invite.

Who calls to me?
Who answers me?

DANS LA NUIT
Henri Michaux

Dans la nuit
Dans la nuit
Je me suis uni à la nuit
A la nuit sans limites
A la nuit.

Mienne, belle, mienne.

Nuit
Nuit de naissance
Qui m'emplis de mon cri
De mes épis
Toi qui m'envahis
Qui fait houle houle
Qui fait houle tout autour
Et fume, es fort dense
Et mugis
Es la nuit
Nuit qui gît, Nuit implacable.
Et sa fanfare, et sa plage
Sa plage en haut, sa plage partout,
Sa plage boit, son poids est roi, et tout ploie sous lui

Sous lui, sous plus ténu qu'un fil
Sous la nuit
La Nuit.

L'Espace du dedans. 1944

IN THE NIGHT

In the night
In the night
I am united to the night
To the infinite night
To the night.

Mine, lovely, mine.
Night
Night of life
You fill me with my cry
You inspire me
You invade me
You surge surge
You surge around
You are deep mist
And you wail
You are night
Prostrate, implacable night.
And her flourish, and her shore
Her shore on high, shore everywhere,
Her shore drinks, its weight is king, all sinks

Beneath it, tighter than wire
Beneath the night
The Night.

LE DERNIER POEME
Robert Desnos

J'ai rêvé tellement fort de toi,
J'ai tellement marché, tellement parlé,
Tellement aimé ton ombre,
Qu'il ne me reste plus rien de toi.
Il me reste d'être l'ombre parmi les ombres
D'être cent fois plus ombre que l'ombre
D'être l'ombre qui viendra et reviendra dans ta vie
   ensoleillée.

<u>Domaine public.</u> 1945

THE LAST POEM

I've dreamed so vividly of you,
I've walked so far, and talked so much,
And I've so deeply loved your shadow
That I have nothing left of you.
I am only a shade among the shades,
A hundred times more shadowy than shade,
I am the shadow that will come and go in your sunny life.

PLEIN CIEL
Jules Supervielle

J'avais un cheval
Dans un champ de ciel
Et je m'enfonçais
Dans le jour ardent.
Rien ne m'arrêtait
J'allais sans savoir,
C'était un navire
Plutôt qu'un cheval,
C'était un désir
Plutôt qu'un navire,
C'était un cheval
Comme on n'en voit pas,
Tête de coursier,
Robe de délire,
Un vent qui hennit
En se répandant.

Je montais toujours
Et faisais des signes:
"Suivez mon chemin,
Vous pouvez venir,
Mes meilleurs amis,
La route est sereine,
Le ciel est ouvert.
Mais qui parle ainsi ?
Je me perds de vue
Dans cette altitude,
Me distinguez-vous ?
Je suis celui qui
Parlait tout à l'heure,
Suis-je encor celui
Qui parle à présent,
Vous-mêmes, amis,
Etes-vous les mêmes ?
L'un efface l'autre
Et change en montant."

<u>1939-45.</u> 1946

HIGH IN THE SKY

I once had a horse
In a field of sky
And I used to plunge
In the burning day.
Nothing would stop me
Unknowing I moved,
It was a swift ship
Instead of a horse,
It was a desire
Instead of a ship,
Or the sort of horse
That one never sees,
With a charger's head,
Delirious coat,
An expanding wind
That whinnied and neighed.

I would always mount
And beckon and call:
"Come follow my path,
Do not hesitate,
My very good friends,
The way is serene,
The sky is quite clear.
But who speaks these words?
I lose sight of me
At this altitude,
Can you make me out?
I am the one who
Was speaking just now,
Am I also the one
Who is speaking here,
And yourselves, my friends,
Are you still the same?
We renew ourselves
And change as we mount."

POUR TOI MON AMOUR
Jacques Prévert

Je suis allé au marché aux oiseaux
    Et j'ai acheté des oiseaux
        Pour toi
      mon amour
Je suis allé au marché aux fleurs
    Et j'ai acheté des fleurs
        Pour toi
      mon amour
Je suis allé au marché à la ferraille
    Et j'ai acheté des chaînes
      De lourdes chaînes
        Pour toi
      mon amour
Et puis je suis allé au marché aux esclaves
    Et je t'ai cherchée
  Mais je ne t'ai pas trouvée
      mon amour.

Paroles.   1946

FOR YOU MY LOVE

I went to the shop where birds are sold
    And I bought some birds
        For you
      my love
I went to the shop where flowers are sold
    And I bought some flowers
        For you
      my love
I went to the shop where old iron is sold
    And I bought some chains
    Some heavy chains
        For you
      my love
Then I went to the shop where slaves are sold
    And I searched for you
    But I did not find you there
      my love.

RUE DE SEINE
Jacques Prévert

Rue de Seine dix heures et demie
le soir
au coin d'une autre rue
un homme titube ... un homme jeune
avec un chapeau
un imperméable
une femme le secoue ...
elle le secoue
et elle lui parle
et il secoue la tête
son chapeau est tout de travers
et le chapeau de la femme s'apprête à tomber en arrière
ils sont très pâles tous les deux
l'homme certainement a envie de partir ...
de disparaître ... de mourir ...
mais la femme a une furieuse envie de vivre
et sa voix
sa voix qui chuchote
on ne peut pas ne pas l'entendre
c'est une plainte ...
un ordre ...
un cri ...
tellement avide cette voix ...
et triste
et vivante ...
un nouveau-né malade qui grelotte sur une tombe
dans un cimetière l'hiver ...
le cri d'un être les doigts pris dans la portière ...
une chanson
une phrase
toujours la même
une phrase
répétée ...
sans arrêt
sans réponse ...
l'homme la regarde ses yeux tournent
il fait des gestes avec les bras
comme un noyé
et la phrase revient
rue de Seine au coin d'une autre rue

RUE DE SEINE

Rue de Seine ten thirty
evening
at the corner of the street
a man is reeling ... a young man
with a hat
a raincoat
a woman is shaking him
she shakes him
and speaks to him
and he is shaking his head
his hat is askew
and the woman's hat is almost falling off the back of her head
they are both very pale
the man obviously wants to get away ...
to disappear ... to die ...
but the woman has a furious desire to live
and her voice
her whispering voice
one cannot avoid hearing it
is a complaint ...
a command ...
a cry ...
so greedy this voice
and sad
and alive ...
a sickly newborn baby shivering on a tombstone
in a cemetery in winter ...
the cry of a person whose fingers are caught in the car door ...
a song
a sentence
always the same one
a sentence
repeated ...
without pause
without answer ...
the man looks at her looks away
he gestures with his arms
like a drowning man
and the sentence comes again
rue de Seine at the corner of the street

la femme continue
sans se lasser ...
continue sa question inquiète
plaie impossible à panser
Pierre dis-moi la vérité
Pierre dis-moi la vérité
je veux tout savoir
dis-moi la vérité ...
le chapeau de la femme tombe
Pierre je veux tout savoir
dis-moi la vérité
question stupide et grandiose
Pierre ne sait que répondre
il est perdu
celui qui s'appelle Pierre ...
il a un sourire que peut-être il voudrait tendre
et répète
Voyons calme-toi tu es folle
mais il ne croit pas si bien dire
mais il ne voit pas
il ne peut pas voir comment
sa bouche d'homme est tordue par son sourire ...
il étouffe
le monde se couche sur lui
et l'étouffe
il est prisonnier
coincé par ses promesses ...
on lui demande des comptes ...
en face de lui ...
une machine à compter
une machine à écrire des lettres d'amour
une machine à souffrir
le saisit ...
s'accroche à lui ...
Pierre dis-moi la vérité.

Paroles. 1946

the woman continues
tirelessly ...
continues her anxious questioning
a wound impossible to dress
Pierre tell me the truth
Pierre tell me the truth
I want to know all
tell me the truth ...
the woman's hat falls off
Pierre I want to know all
tell me the truth ...
stupid and ambitious question
Pierre doesn't know what to answer
he is lost
the man named Pierre
he smiles in a way that he means perhaps to be affectionate
and repeats
Come now calm down you are crazy
he speaks more truly than he knows
but he doesn't see
he cannot see how
his mouth is twisted by his smile ...
he is being smothered
the world is bearing down upon him
smothering him
he is a prisoner
wedged between his promises ...
he is being called to account
face to face
an adding machine
a machine for writing love letters
a machine for suffering
is seizing him ...
is clinging to him ...
Pierre tell me the truth.

LE LORIOT
René Char

3 septembre 1939

Le loriot entra dans la capitale de l'aube.
L'épée de son chant ferma le lit triste.
Tout à jamais prit fin.

Fureur et mystère. 1948

THE ORIOLE

September 3, 1939

The oriole entered the capital of dawn.
The blade of its song closed the sad bed.
Everything came to an end.

S. O. S.
Yvan Goll

L'appel inaudible de ton âme
Je le sens par-dessus toutes les mers.
Il me frappe comme un radiogramme divin,
Les oiseaux l'écrivent dans le zénith,
La pluie le frappe en morse à ma fenêtre,
Les arbres le chuchotent dans les parcs ...
J'interromps toute affaire,
La bourse des poètes ferme,
Le soleil tombe:
Je viens.

L'antirose. 1965

S. O. S.

Across the oceans I receive
The soundless summons of your soul.
Like a divine radiogram it reaches me.
Birds write it in the zenith,
Rain taps it out in morse on my window,
In the park trees whisper it ...
I abandon all business,
The poets' exchange closes,
The sun falls:
I am coming.

ROSE DE SANG
Yvan Goll

Tous les arbres de l'hiver
Avaient déjà oublié leurs noms et leurs oiseaux
Ils attendaient comme des mendiants dans la forêt

Et un buisson se dressait dans le vent
Plus pauvre et plus maigre qu'eux tous
Il avait les bras les plus décharnés

Mais quand j'approchai
Pour caresser une de ses branches
Il saigna tout à coup

Et dans cette grande goutte rouge
Se formèrent des roses rondes
Ainsi saignent les saints et les amants

L'antirose.   1965

BLOOD ROSE

All the trees of winter
Had already forgotten their names and their birds
They were waiting like beggars in the forest

And a bush was standing in the wind
Poorer and thinner than the others
Its arms were nakedest of all

But when I approached
To stroke one of its branches
It suddenly bled

And in this great red drop
Round roses formed
So saints and lovers bleed

LETTRE DU VINGT-SIX JUIN
Philippe Jaccottet

Que les oiseaux vous parlent désormais de notre vie.
Un homme en ferait trop d'histoires
et vous ne verriez plus à travers ses paroles
qu'une chambre de voyageur, une fenêtre
où la buée des larmes voile un bois brisé de pluie ...

La nuit se fait. Vous entendez les voix sous les tilleuls:
la voix humaine brille comme au-dessus de la terre
Antarès qui est tantôt rouge et tantôt vert.

*

N'écoutez plus le bruit de nos soucis,
ne pensez plus à ce qui nous arrive,
oubliez même notre nom. Ecoutez-nous parler
avec la voix du jour, et laissez seulement
briller le jour. Quand nous serons défaits de toute crainte,
quand la mort ne sera pour nous que transparence,
quand elle sera claire comme l'air des nuits d'été
et quand nous volerons portés par la légèreté
à travers tous ces illusoires murs que le vent pousse,
vous n'entendrez plus que le bruit de la rivière
qui coule derrière la forêt; et vous ne verrez plus
qu'étinceler des yeux de nuit ...

*

Lorsque nous parlerons avec la voix du rossignol ...

L'Ignorant. 1952-56

LETTER OF JUNE 26th

Henceforth let only birds discuss our life with you
A man would multiply the complications
and through his words you'd see
nothing but a hotel room, a window
where misty tears obscure a grove shattered by rain ...

Night comes on. You hear voices under the linden-trees:
the human voice shines as in the sky
Antares shines now green now red.

Stop listening to the clamor of our cares,
don't dwell upon what's happening to us,
forget even our name. Listen to us speaking
with the voice of day, and give the day
a chance to shine. When we shall be loosed from fear,
when we can see death as a transparency,
as clear as the air of a summer night,
and when we fly on agile wings
through all these phantom walls pushed by the wind,
you will hear only the sound of the stream
flowing beyond the woods; and you will see nothing
but the sparkle of night's eyes ...

When we shall be speaking with the nightingale's voice ...

NOTE ABOUT THE TRANSLATOR

Dorothy Brown Aspinwall (now Mrs. Robert F. Herpick in private life) is Professor of European Languages and chairman of the Division of French at the University of Hawaii where she has taught since 1948. Born in Regina, Canada, Dr. Aspinwall studied at the University of Alberta, the University of Toronto, the Sorbonne, and the University of Washington. Her translation of Charles Péguy's long poem, le porche du mystère de la deuxième vertu, was published by the Scarecrow Press in 1970. She is now completing an anthology of twentieth-century French poetry for classroom use.

OHIO UNIVERSITY LIBRARY

Please return this book as soon as you have finished with it. In order to avoid a fine it must be returned by the latest date stamped below.

PQ
1183
A8